Weird Wonders of the Deep
An Imagination Library Series

Giant Tubeworms

by Valerie J. Weber

GARETH**STEVENS**
PUBLISHING
A WRC Media Company

Please visit our web site at: www.garethstevens.com
For a free color catalog describing Gareth Stevens Publishing's
list of high-quality books and multimedia programs,
call 1-800-542-2595 (USA) or 1-800-387-3178 (Canada).
Gareth Stevens Publishing's fax: (414) 332-3567.

Library of Congress Cataloging-in-Publication Data

Weber, Valerie.
    Giant tubeworms / by Valerie J. Weber.
        p. cm. — (Weird wonders of the deep: an imagination library series)
    Includes bibliographical references and index.
    ISBN 0-8368-4562-5 (lib. bdg.)
    1. Tube worms—Juvenile literature. I. Title.
QL391.A6W43   2005
592'.62—dc22   2004060662

First published in 2005 by
Gareth Stevens Publishing
A WRC Media Company
330 West Olive Street, Suite 100
Milwaukee, WI 53212 USA

Cover design and page layout: Scott M. Krall
Series editors: JoAnn Early Macken and Mark J. Sachner
Picture Researcher: Diane Laska-Swanke

Photo credits: Cover, pp. 7, 11, 15, 17, 19 © Peter Batson/ExploreTheAbyss.Com; pp. 5, 9, 13, 21
© Science VU/Visuals Unlimited

Printed in the United States of America

1 2 3 4 5 6 7 8 9 09 08 07 06 05

Front cover: In one kind of tubeworm, the
chitin forms into hard rings. Minerals from the
vent smoke dye their tubes orange.

Table of Contents

Words that appear in the glossary are printed in **boldface** type the first time they occur in the text.

A Hot Spot in a Cold Place

As the tiny **submersible** sinks down, the sea gets darker. Into the icy depths it falls, farther and farther. Suddenly, a tall shape looms in the distance. A huge chimney rises from the ocean floor. Smoke pours from the chimney, formed from a **hydrothermal vent**.

The water around the chimney shimmers with heat. Bits of plants and dead fish drift down like white flakes in a snow globe.

Strange creatures poke up from the ocean floor. Their white tubes sway gently. A red plume tips each tube. These are tubeworms, living near the hottest place on the ocean floor.

A crab crawls among the tubeworms. Tubeworms look more like strange plants than animals.

A Bearded Worm

As fish and crabs swim close to nibble at the animal's plume, it disappears, sucked back into the tube. The plume looks like a red beard made of two hundred thousand **tentacles**.

The tube itself is made of chitin. A tough material like your fingernails, chitin protects the tubeworm from **predators**.

The bottom of the tubeworm is attached to the sea floor, inches from the hydrothermal vent. Water gushing from the hydrothermal vent reaches 752° Fahrenheit (400° Celsius). The water cools as it leaves the vent. Less than 1 inch (2.5 centimeters) away, the temperature drops to 36° F (2° C).

Deep in the Pacific Ocean, two kinds of giant tubeworms live near cracks in the sea floor. Hot water gushes from these cracks.

Heat in the Deep

Scientists did not discover tubeworms — or hydrothermal vents — until 1977. Traveling in a submersible to more than one and a half miles (2.4 kilometers) down in the Pacific Ocean, they found a hot, weird landscape. Melted rock and smoke gushed from huge towers in the ocean floor.

Hydrothermal vents are formed when seawater trickles deep inside cracks in the ocean floor. The inside of Earth is very hot and heats the water. The hot water rises and dissolves minerals and **chemicals** in the rocks that it passes. As the hot water meets the cold water of the ocean depths, the minerals harden and pile up.

Smoke billows out from a vent in the Pacific Ocean. Two hundred to three hundred vents can grow in an area the size of a football field.

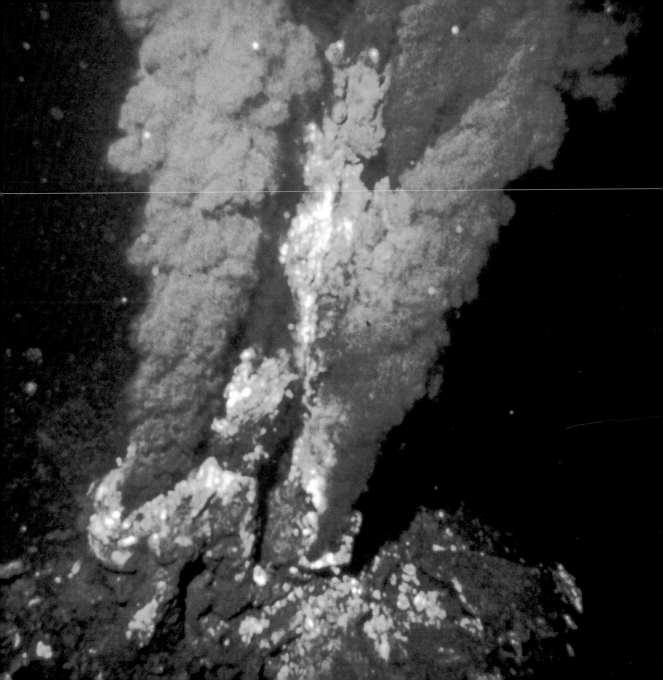

No Mouth? No Stomach? No Problem.

When scientists took apart the tubeworm, they found something shocking. The animal had no mouth, no stomach, and no **gut**! How did it eat? What did it live on?

They were amazed to find the worms carried their food source inside them. How did they do it? Using their plumes, the tubeworms gathered the chemicals from the water pouring from the hydrothermal vents. These chemicals would kill most other animals. (Plus they really stink!) Tiny **bacteria** inside the tubeworms turned the chemicals into food for their hosts. In turn, the tubeworms provided a safe place for the bacteria to live and grow.

Plumes like feathers peek from the tubeworm's tip. Tubeworm plumes are red because they are filled with blood.

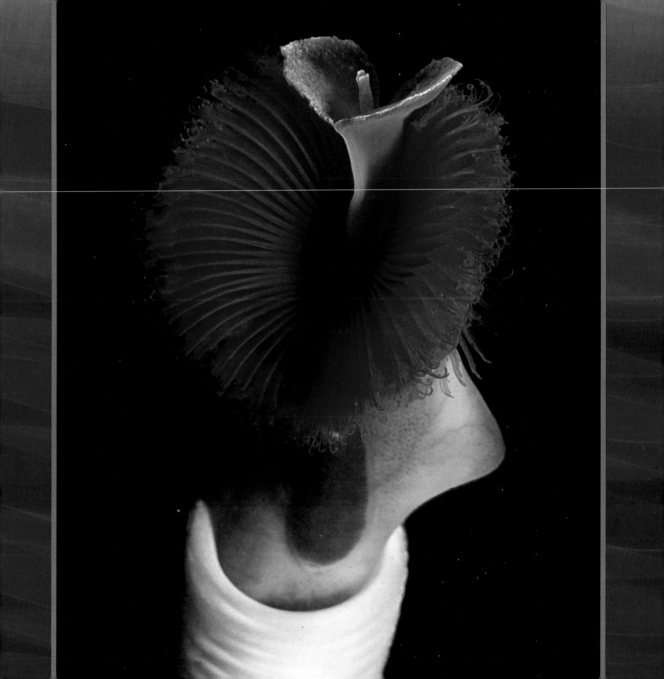

Friends Inside Help

More questions remained. How did the tube-worms get the bacteria inside them if they had no mouths?

Scientists looked to the tubeworm's earliest life. When a tubeworm first hatches from its egg, it has a mouth and a stomach. As it swims near the hydrothermal vent, it draws the special bacteria inside its mouth and swallows them. As the tube-worm ages, its stomach closes with the bacteria inside. Its mouth disappears.

The tubeworm attaches itself to the ocean floor near the hydrothermal vent. There, the bacteria inside have plenty of chemicals to use.

Living and dead tubeworms stand on the ocean floor. It takes a long time for dead animals to rot on the ocean floor.

A Shaky Home

Tubeworms thrive near the vents, shooting up to 8 feet (nearly 3 meters) tall. They can grow up to 33 inches (84 centimeters) each year.

The ground underneath the tubeworms shakes and shimmies. The chimneys can grow quickly, up to nearly 20 feet (6 m) in one year. They can also fall fast. The tubeworm and its bacteria can live as long as the hydrothermal vent lasts. Without an active vent and its chemicals, the tubeworms die off.

Larval tubeworms can float away from their parents on ocean **currents**. They can live up to thirty-eight days without food so they can drift to another hydrothermal vent many miles away.

A tubeworm's plume can grow to the size of a human hand. The slit in the side of the plume releases tubeworm eggs.

Life in the Neighborhood

While the neighborhood maybe hot and **unstable**, other creatures crowd alongside the tubeworm. Pompeii worms live even closer to the heat than tubeworms. They can stand water up to 176° F (80° C). Pompeii worms also live in tubes, but their heads are shaped like stars with many points.

Eelpouts wind among the tubeworms. Unlike most fish, eelpouts have skin, not **scales**. These long, slim fish are ghostly white. They are among the few fish that can live so deep in the sea.

While a Pompeii worm's rear sits in water as hot as 176° F (80° C), its head stays in cooler water of about 72° F (22° C). The fur on its back is actually formed from bacteria.

Tubeworm Neighbors

Giant white clams the size of dinner plates also settle at hydrothermal vents. Bacteria in their **gills** make food for them as well.

Tubeworm predators live alongside the tubeworms. As an adult, the hydrothermal vent crab is white as a ghost. It grows up to 5 inches (11 cm) long. As a youngster, the crab is bright red and less than an inch (2.5 cm) long. Both sizes feed on the red tip of the tubeworm — if they can catch it.

This hydrothermal vent crab climbs over the hardened rock at the base of the vent. It can live in waters ranging from 77° F (25° C) to 36° F (2° C).

A Life without Sun

Most plants and animals need the Sun in some way to survive. Plants need sunlight to grow. Most animals live either by eating plants or by eating other animals that eat plants. Sunlight cannot reach deep into the ocean, so plants cannot grow there. Many deep-sea animals eat bits of dead animals and plants floating down from above. So far, hydrothermal vent animals living off bacteria are the only ones known who do not need the Sun, plants, or animals that eat plants to survive.

We have only explored one one-hundredth of the deep sea. What other odd creatures besides tubeworms and their neighbors may survive in strange ways there?

Mussels, giant tubeworms, and crabs crowd together around a hydrothermal vent. Scientists have discovered over three hundred new kinds of animals at hydrothermal vents. Many are found nowhere else, and most could not live away from the vents.

More to Read and View

Books (Nonfiction)

The Deep Sea Floor. Sneed B. Collard (Charlesbridge Publishing)
Destination — Deep Sea. Jonathan Grupper (National Geographic Society)
Eyewitness: Ocean. Miranda MacQuitty (DK Publishing)
Groovy Tube Books: Sea Splash. Stephanie Fitzgerald (Innovative Kids)

Videos (Nonfiction)

Volcanoes of the Deep. (Nova)
Volcanoes of the Deep Sea. (Steven Low Distribution)

Places to Write and Visit

Here are three places to contact for more information:

American Museum of Natural History
Central Park West at 79th Street
New York, NY 10024
1-212-765-5100
www.amnh.org

Field Museum of Natural History
1400 South Lake Shore Drive
Chicago, IL 60605-2496
1-312-922-9410
www.fieldmuseum.org

Smithsonian National Museum of Natural History
10th Street and Constitution Avenue, NW
Washington, D.C. 20560
1-202-633-1000
www.mnh.si.edu

Web Sites

Web sites change frequently, but we believe the following web sites are going to last. You can also use good search engines, such as **Yahooligans!** [www.yahooligans.com] or **Google** [www.google.com], to find more information about giant tubeworms. Here are some keywords to help you: *hydrothermal vents*, *Pompeii worms*, *eelpouts*, and *giant white clams*.

projects.edtech.sandi.net/miramesa/Organelles/vents.html

Follow the links on this web site to learn more about hydrothermal vents and the animals that live near them.

www.ocean.udel.edu/deepsea/level-2/creature/tube.html

Visit this site to see a short video about tubeworm and other deep sea creatures in action and learn more about these dwellers on the ocean floor.

yucky.kids.discovery.com/flash/worm/pg000217.html

Wendall the worm interviews Bobby the Bearded Worm, a tubeworm, about his life and environment.

Glossary

You can find these words on the pages listed. Reading a word in a sentence helps you understand it even better.

bacteria (baK-TEER-ee-uh) — tiny, one-celled, living beings 10, 12, 14, 18, 20

chemicals (KEM-ih-kuhls) — solids, liquids, or gases. A chemical can be a mix of different elements or the same throughout. Everything is made of chemicals. 8, 10, 12, 14

currents (KUR-uhnts) — a part of a body of water that moves along a specific path 14

gills (GILS) — the part of a fish used for breathing. Gills take in oxygen from the water. 18

gut (GUHT) — intestines that absorb energy from food and take waste out of the body 10

hydrothermal vent (hi-droh-THUR-muhl VENT) — crack in Earth's surface where hot water comes out 4, 6, 8, 10, 12, 14, 18, 20

larval (LAHR-vuhl) — in a newly hatched, earliest stage of a fish or insect, often looking like a worm 14

minerals (MIN-ur-uhls) — substances that are not plants or animals 2, 8

predators (PRED-uh-turz) — animals that hunt other animals for food 6, 18

scales (SKAYLZ) — small, stiff plates that cover a fish, snake, or lizard's skin 16

submersible (sub-MER-si-buhl) — a ship that can go deep underwater 4, 8

tentacles (TEN-tuh-kuhls) long, thin growths from an animal's body that bend easily. Squids and octopuses also have tentacles. 6

unstable (un-STAY-buhl) — easily moved, likely to change 16

Index